MARKS & SPENCER

stir-fry

simple and delicious easy-to-make recipes

Marks and Spencer p.l.c.
PO Box 3339,
Chester, CH99 9QS

www.marksandspencer.com

ISBN: 1-84461-490-5

Printed in China

This edition designed by Talking Design, Worthing

NOTES FOR THE READER

- This book uses both metric and imperial measurements. Follow the same units of measurement throughout; do not mix metric and imperial.
- All spoon measurements are level: teaspoons are assumed to be 5 ml, and tablespoons are assumed to be 15 ml.
- Unless otherwise stated, milk is assumed to be full fat, eggs and individual vegetables such as potatoes are medium, and pepper is freshly ground black pepper.
- Recipes using raw or very lightly cooked eggs should be avoided by infants, the elderly, pregnant women, convalescents, and anyone suffering from an illness.
- Optional ingredients, variations or serving suggestions have not been included in the calculations.
- The times given are an approximate guide only. Preparation times differ according to the techniques used by different people and the cooking times vary as a result of the type of oven used.

contents

introduction

Stir-fries are generally fast, tasty and highly nutritional meals. Only small quantities of meat are used compared with traditional Western cooking, and the healthy emphasis on vegetables, together with accompanying rice and noodles, means they are good for you, too.

Stir-frying is ideal for the busy cook – most recipes are very easy to prepare and quick to cook. And you can be guaranteed to find something in this book to please all tastes, with a wide range of recipes from the Far East, some with Chinese influence and others with spicy Thai and Indian derivation.

The recipes have been divided into four sections – Chicken & Turkey, Fish & Seafood, Beef & Pork, and Vegetables – for ease of reference. You will find that once your confidence grows in this style of cooking, you will enjoy experimenting with ingredients (for example, substituting one kind of meat for another) to suit your own personal tastes.

Stir-frying is a highly versatile and adaptable style of cooking that is great for the bold and imaginative cook. Experiment and enjoy!

guide to recipe key

CATEGORY
Recipes are graded as follows:
1 pea = easy, 2 peas = very easy, 3 peas = extremely easy.

SERVES 4
Recipes generally serve four people. Simply halve the ingredients to serve two, taking care not to mix imperial and metric measurements.

10 MINUTES
Preparation time.

10 MINUTES
Cooking time.

chicken
& turkey

Chicken and turkey offer healthy meat options and are very tasty in a wide range of stir-fry dishes – from Turkey, Broccoli & Pak Choi to Chicken with Shiitake Mushrooms. Included in this section are some traditional favourites, such as Chicken Fried Rice, to some more exotic recipes for the bolder cook, such as Turkey with Bamboo Shoots and Water Chestnuts.

VERY EASY   SERVES 4   10 MINUTES +
2 HOURS TO
MARINATE   9 MINUTES

turkey, broccoli & pak choi

MARINADE
1 tbsp soy sauce
1 tbsp honey
2 cloves garlic, crushed
STIR-FRY
450 g/1 lb turkey breast,
  cut into strips

1 tbsp vegetable oil
1 head of broccoli,
  cut into florets
2 heads of pak choi,
  leaves washed and
  separated (or savoy
  cabbage, if pak choi is
  unavailable)

1 red pepper, sliced thinly
50 ml/2 fl oz chicken
  stock
cooked rice, to serve

In a medium-sized bowl, stir together the soy sauce, honey and garlic.
Add the turkey and toss to coat. Cover the bowl with clingfilm and
refrigerate for 2 hours to marinate.

Put a wok or large frying pan over a medium-high heat and add the oil;
heat for 1 minute. Add the turkey and stir-fry for 3 minutes, or until the
turkey is opaque. Remove with a slotted spoon, set aside and keep warm.

Add the broccoli, pak choi (or savoy cabbage) and the pepper to the pan
and stir-fry for 2 minutes. Add the stock and continue to stir-fry for
2 minutes, or until the vegetables are crisp yet tender.

Return the turkey to the pan and cook briefly to reheat. Serve
immediately with hot rice.

pad thai noodles

225 g/9 oz rice noodles
90 g/3½ oz peanuts,
  chopped roughly
2 tbsp lime juice
1 tbsp caster sugar
6 tbsp fish sauce
1 tsp hot chilli sauce,
  or to taste
250 g/9 oz firm tofu,
  cubed

vegetable oil, for deep
  frying
3 tbsp peanut oil
1 garlic clove, crushed
1 onion, sliced finely
1 red pepper, sliced thinly
250 g/9 oz chicken
  breast, cut into thin
  strips
90 g/3½ oz beansprouts
125 g/4½ oz mangetouts

175 g/6 oz prawns,
  peeled, cut in half
  lengthways
3 eggs, beaten
1 lemon, cut into wedges,
  4 spring onions, chopped
  finely, 2 tbsp chopped
  peanuts, and 1 tbsp
  chopped fresh basil,
  to serve

Soak the noodles in a bowl of warm water for about 20 minutes, or until soft. Drain thoroughly in a colander and set aside. In a small bowl, combine the peanuts, lime juice, sugar, fish sauce and hot chilli sauce and set aside.

Rinse the tofu in cold water, place between layers of kitchen paper and pat dry. Heat the oil for deep-frying in a large frying pan or wok. Deep-fry the tofu over a medium heat for 2 minutes until light brown and crisp. Remove from the heat, lift tofu out with a slotted spoon and set aside on kitchen paper to drain.

Heat a large frying pan or wok and add the peanut oil, garlic, onion, red pepper and chicken strips. Cook for 2–3 minutes. Stir in the beansprouts and mangetouts and cook for 1 minute. Then add the prawns, noodles, eggs and tofu and stir-fry for 4–5 minutes. Finally, add the peanut and lime juice mixture and cook for 3–4 minutes. Transfer to warm dishes, garnish and serve.

chicken & shiitake mushrooms

MARINADE
175 g/6 oz white sugar
225 ml/8 fl oz soy sauce
1 tsp Chinese five spice
 powder
225 ml/8 fl oz sweet
 sherry

STIR-FRY
2 tbsp vegetable oil
675 g/1½ lb chicken
 breast, skinned and cut
 into 2.5 cm/1 inch chunks
1 tsp grated fresh root
 ginger
3 carrots, sliced thinly

2 onions, sliced thinly
100 g/3½ oz beansprouts
225 g/8 oz fresh or dried
 shiitake mushrooms,
 sliced thinly
3 tbsp chopped fresh
 coriander
cooked noodles, to serve

Combine the sugar, soy sauce, Chinese five spice powder and sweet
sherry in a bowl. Mix well and set aside.

In a frying pan or wok, heat the oil over a medium-high heat. Add the
chicken and stir-fry for 2 minutes, then add the ginger and fry for
1 minute, stirring continuously. Add the marinade and cook for 2 more
minutes.

One at a time add the carrots, onions, beansprouts, mushrooms and
coriander. Stir-fry after each addition.

Once the marinade has reduced and is thick, transfer the stir-fry
to warm serving bowls. Serve hot with boiled noodles.

EXTREMELY EASY SERVES 4 10 MINUTES + 1 HOUR TO MARINATE   9 MINUTES

ginger chicken with toasted sesame seeds

MARINADE
4 tbsp soy sauce
4 tbsp water
STIR-FRY
500 g/1 lb 2 oz chicken
  breasts, skinned,
  cut into strips

2 tbsp groundnut oil
1 leek, sliced thinly
1 head of broccoli,
  cut into small florets
2 carrots, sliced thinly
½ cauliflower, cut into
  small florets

1 tsp grated fresh root
  ginger
5 tbsp white wine
2 tbsp sesame seeds
1 tbsp cornflour
1 tbsp water
cooked rice, to serve

In a medium dish, combine the soy sauce with 4 tablespoons of water. Toss and coat the chicken strips in the sauce. Cover the dish with clingfilm and refrigerate for 1 hour.

Remove the chicken from the marinade with a slotted spoon. Heat the oil in a frying pan or wok, and stir-fry the chicken and leek until the chicken is browned and the leek is beginning to soften.

Stir in the vegetables, ginger and wine. Reduce the heat, cover and simmer for 5 minutes.

Place the sesame seeds on a baking sheet under a hot grill. Stir them once to make sure they toast evenly. Set aside to cool.

In a small bowl, combine the cornflour with 1 tablespoon of water and whisk until smooth. Gradually add the liquid to the frying pan, stirring constantly until thickened.

Pile onto a bed of hot rice, top with the sesame seeds and serve.

turkey with bamboo shoots & water chestnuts

MARINADE
4 tbsp sweet sherry
1 tbsp lemon juice
1 tbsp soy sauce
2 tsp grated fresh root
　ginger
1 clove garlic, crushed

STIR-FRY
450 g/1 lb turkey breast,
　cubed
1 tbsp sesame oil
2 tbsp vegetable oil
125 g/4½ oz small
　mushrooms, cut into
　halves
1 green pepper, cut into
　strips

1 courgette, sliced thinly
4 spring onions, cut into
　quarters
115 g/4 oz canned
　bamboo shoots, drained
115 g/4 oz canned sliced
　water chestnuts, drained
cooked noodles, to serve

Blend the sherry, lemon juice, soy sauce, ginger and garlic in a bowl, then add the turkey and stir. Cover the dish with clingfilm and refrigerate to marinate for 3–4 hours.

In a wok or frying pan, add the sesame oil and vegetable oil and heat slowly. Remove the turkey from the marinade with a slotted spoon (reserving the marinade) and stir-fry a few pieces at a time until browned. Remove the turkey from the pan and set aside.

Add the mushrooms, green pepper and courgette to the pan and stir-fry for 3 minutes. Add the spring onions and stir-fry for 1 minute more. Add the bamboo shoots and water chestnuts to the pan, then the turkey along with half of the reserved marinade. Stir over a medium-high heat for another 2–3 minutes, until the ingredients are evenly coated and the marinade has reduced.

Serve immediately over noodles or rice.

hot & spicy chicken with peanuts

MARINADE
2 tbsp soy sauce
1 tsp chilli powder
  (or to taste)
STIR-FRY
350 g/12 oz chicken
  breasts, skinned and cut
  into chunks

4 tbsp peanut oil
1 clove garlic, chopped
  finely
1 tsp grated fresh root
  ginger
3 shallots, sliced thinly
225 g/8 oz carrots,
  sliced thinly

1 tsp white wine vinegar
pinch of sugar
90 g/3¼ oz roasted
  peanuts
1 tbsp groundnut oil
rice and coriander,
  to serve

Mix the soy sauce and chilli powder in a bowl. Add the chicken chunks and toss to coat. Cover with clingfilm and refrigerate for 30 minutes.

Heat the oil in a frying pan or wok, and stir-fry the chicken until browned and well cooked. Remove from the pan, set aside and keep warm.

If necessary, add a little more oil to the pan, then add the garlic, ginger, shallots and carrots. Stir-fry for 2–3 minutes.

Return the chicken to the pan and fry until it is warmed through. Add the vinegar, sugar and peanuts, stir well and drizzle with the groundnut oil.

Serve immediately with rice and coriander.

lemon turkey with spinach

MARINADE

1 tbsp soy sauce

1 tbsp white wine vinegar

1 tsp cornflour

1 tsp finely grated lemon zest

½ tsp finely ground black pepper

STIR-FRY

450 g/1 lb turkey breast, cut into strips

1 tbsp vegetable oil

6 spring onions, sliced finely

½ lemon, peeled and sliced thinly

1 garlic clove, chopped finely

300 g/10½ oz spinach, washed, drained and chopped roughly

3 tbsp chopped fresh flat-leaf parsley

lemon slices, to garnish

sprigs of flat-leaf parsley, to garnish

500 g/1 lb 2 oz cooked tagliatelle or fettucine, to serve

Put the soy sauce, vinegar, cornflour, lemon zest and pepper in a bowl and mix thoroughly. Add the turkey and stir to coat. Cover with clingfilm and marinate in the refrigerator for 30 minutes.

Heat the oil in a large wok or frying pan. Add the turkey and the marinade and cook over a medium heat for 2–3 minutes, or until the turkey is opaque.

Add the spring onions, lemon slivers and garlic and cook for another 2–3 minutes. Stir in the spinach and parsley and cook until the spinach is just wilted.

Remove from the heat, spoon over the hot pasta and garnish with sprigs of parsley and lemon slices before serving.

chicken with pistachio nuts

50 ml/2 fl oz chicken
  stock
2 tbsp soy sauce
2 tbsp dry sherry
3 tsp cornflour
1 egg white, beaten
½ tsp salt
4 tbsp peanut or
  vegetable oil

450 g/1 lb chicken
  breast, cut into strips
450 g/1 lb mushrooms,
  sliced thinly
1 head of broccoli,
  cut into florets
150 g/5½ oz beansprouts

100 g/3½ oz canned
  water chestnuts,
  drained and sliced thinly
175 g/6 oz pistachio nuts,
  plus extra to garnish
  (optional)
boiled white rice, to serve

Combine the chicken stock, soy sauce and sherry with 1 teaspoon of cornflour. Stir well and set aside.

Combine the egg white, salt, 2 tablespoons of the oil and 2 teaspoons of cornflour. Toss and coat the chicken in the mixture.

In a wok or frying pan, heat the remaining vegetable oil until hot. Add the chicken in batches and stir-fry until golden. Remove from the pan, drain on kitchen paper and set aside to keep warm.

Add more oil to the pan if needed and stir-fry the mushrooms, then add the broccoli and cook for 2–3 minutes.

Return the chicken to the pan and add the beansprouts, water chestnuts and pistachio nuts. Stir-fry until all the ingredients are thoroughly warm. Add the chicken stock mixture and cook, stirring continuously until thickened.

Serve immediately over a bed of rice, garnished with pistachios.

chicken fried rice

½ tbsp sesame oil
6 shallots, peeled and
  quartered
450g/1 lb cooked, cubed
  chicken meat
3 tbsp soy sauce
2 carrots, diced
1 stalk celery, diced

1 red pepper, diced
175g/6 oz fresh peas
100 g/3½ oz canned
  sweetcorn
275 g/9½ oz cooked
  long-grain rice
2 large eggs, scrambled

Heat the oil in a large frying pan over a medium heat. Add the shallots
and fry until soft, then add the chicken and 2 tablespoons of the soy
sauce and stir-fry for 5–6 minutes.

Stir in the carrots, celery, red pepper, peas and sweetcorn and
stir-fry for another 5 minutes. Add the rice and stir thoroughly.

Finally, stir in the scrambled eggs and the remaining tablespoon of soy
sauce. Serve immediately.

fish
& seafood

Stir-frying is a great way to prepare fish and seafood because it enhances their delicate texture and subtle flavours. This selection includes spicy options such as Sweet Chilli Squid and Ginger Prawns with Oyster Mushrooms as well as dishes enhanced with herbs, such as Salmon & Scallops with Coriander and Lime – a range of recipes to suit every taste.

VERY EASY   **SERVES 4**   ⌣ **5 MINUTES**   ◷ **4–5 MINUTES**

scallops in black bean sauce

2 tbsp vegetable or
    groundnut oil
1 tsp finely chopped
    garlic
1 tsp finely chopped fresh
    root ginger

1 tbsp fermented black
    beans, rinsed and lightly
    mashed
400 g/14 oz scallops
½ tsp light soy sauce
1 tsp Shaoxing rice wine
1 tsp sugar

3–4 fresh red bird's-eye
    chillies, finely chopped
1–2 tsp chicken stock
1 tbsp finely chopped
    spring onion

In a preheated wok or deep pan, heat the oil. Add the garlic and stir, then add the ginger and stir-fry together for about 1 minute until fragrant. Mix in the black beans, toss in the scallops and stir-fry for 1 minute. Add the light soy sauce, Shaoxing, sugar and chilli.

Lower the heat and simmer for 2 minutes, adding the stock if necessary. Finally add the spring onion, stir and serve.

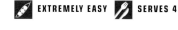
monkfish stir-fry

2 tsp sesame oil
450 g/1 lb monkfish
  steaks, cut into
  2.5 cm/1 inch chunks
1 onion, sliced thinly
3 cloves garlic, chopped
  finely

1 tsp grated fresh root
  ginger
225 g/8 oz fine tip
  asparagus
175 g/6 oz mushrooms,
  sliced thinly
2 tbsp soy sauce

1 tbsp lemon juice
lemon wedges, to garnish
cooked noodles, to serve

Heat the oil in a frying pan over a medium-high heat. Add the fish, onion, garlic, ginger, asparagus and mushrooms. Stir-fry for 2–3 minutes.

Stir in the soy sauce and lemon juice and cook for another minute. Remove from the heat and transfer to warm serving dishes.

Garnish with lemon wedges and serve immediately on a bed of cooked noodles.

VERY EASY   **SERVES 4**   **12 MINUTES**   **9 MINUTES**

prawns, mangetouts & cashew nuts

85 g/3 oz dry roasted cashew nuts
3 tbsp peanut oil
4 spring onions, slivered
2 stalks celery, sliced thinly
3 carrots, sliced finely

100 g/3½ oz baby corn cobs, halved
175 g/6 oz mushrooms, sliced finely
1 clove of garlic, chopped roughly
450 g/1 lb uncooked prawns, peeled

1 tsp cornflour
2 tbsp soy sauce
50 ml/2 fl oz chicken stock
225 g/8 oz savoy cabbage, shredded
175 g/6 oz mangetouts
cooked rice, to serve

Put the frying pan over a medium heat and add the cashew nuts; toast them until they begin to brown. Remove with a slotted spoon and reserve.

Add the oil to the pan and heat. Add the spring onions, celery, carrots and baby corn cobs and cook, stirring occasionally, over a medium-high heat for 3–4 minutes.

Add the mushrooms and cook until they become brown. Mix in the garlic and prawns, stirring until the prawns turn pink.

Mix the cornflour smoothly with the soy sauce and chicken stock. Add the liquid to the shrimp mixture and stir. Then add the savoy cabbage, mangetouts and all but a few of the cashew nuts and cook for 2 minutes.

Garnish with the reserved cashew nuts and serve on a bed of rice.

ginger prawns with oyster mushrooms

150 ml/5 fl oz chicken
  stock
2 tsp sesame seeds
3 tsp grated fresh root
  ginger
1 tbsp soy sauce
¼ tsp hot pepper sauce

1 tsp cornflour
3 tbsp vegetable oil
3 carrots, sliced thinly
350 g/12 oz oyster
  mushrooms, sliced thinly
1 large red pepper, sliced
  thinly

450g/1 lb large prawns,
  peeled
2 garlic cloves, crushed
cooked rice, to serve
coriander, to garnish

In a small bowl, stir together the chicken stock, sesame seeds, ginger, soy sauce, hot pepper sauce and cornflour until well blended. Set aside.

In a large frying pan or wok, heat 2 tablespoons of the oil. Stir-fry the carrots for 3 minutes, remove from the pan and set aside.

Add 1 tablespoon more oil to the pan and fry the mushrooms for 2 minutes. Remove from the pan and set aside.

Add more oil if needed and stir-fry the pepper with the prawns and garlic for 3 minutes, until the prawns turn pink and opaque.

Stir the sauce again and pour it into the frying pan. Cook until the mixture bubbles, then return the carrots and mushrooms to the pan. Cover and cook for 2 minutes longer, until heated through.

Serve over hot cooked rice and garnish with coriander.

salmon & scallops with coriander & lime

6 tbsp groundnut oil
280 g/10 oz salmon
  steak, skinned and cut
  into 2.5 cm/1 inch
  chunks
225 g/8 oz scallops
3 carrots, sliced thinly
2 celery stalks, cut into
  2.5 cm/1 inch pieces

2 yellow peppers, sliced
  thinly
175 g/6 oz oyster
  mushrooms,
  sliced thinly
1 clove garlic, crushed
6 tbsp chopped fresh
  coriander
3 shallots, sliced thinly

2 limes, juiced
1 tsp lime zest
1 tsp dried red pepper
  flakes
3 tbsp dry sherry
3 tbsp soy sauce
cooked noodles, to serve

In a large frying pan or wok, heat the oil over a medium heat. Add the salmon and scallops, and stir-fry for 3 minutes. Remove from the pan, set aside and keep warm.

Add the carrots, celery, peppers, mushrooms and garlic to the pan and stir-fry for 3 minutes. Add the coriander and shallots, and stir.

Add the lime juice and zest, dried red pepper flakes, sherry and soy sauce and stir. Return the salmon and scallops to the pan and stir-fry carefully for another minute.

Serve immediately on a bed of cooked noodles.

sweet chilli squid

1 tbsp sesame seeds,
  toasted
2 tbsp sesame oil
280 g/10 oz squid, cut
  into strips
2 red peppers, sliced
  thinly

3 shallots, sliced thinly
85 g/3 oz mushrooms,
  sliced thinly
1 tbsp dry sherry
4 tbsp soy sauce
1 tsp sugar

1 tsp hot chilli flakes,
  or to taste
1 clove of garlic, crushed
1 tsp sesame oil
cooked rice, to serve

Place the sesame seeds on a baking sheet, toast under a hot grill and set aside. Heat 1 tablespoon of oil in a frying pan over a medium heat. Add the squid and cook for 2 minutes. Remove from the pan and set aside.

Add the other tablespoon of oil to the pan and fry the peppers and shallots over a medium heat for 1 minute. Add the mushrooms and fry for another 2 minutes.

Return the squid to the pan and add the sherry, soy sauce, sugar, chilli flakes and garlic, stirring thoroughly. Cook for a further 2 minutes.

Sprinkle with the toasted sesame seeds, drizzle over 1 tsp sesame oil and mix. Serve on a bed of rice.

prawns with spring onions and straw mushrooms

2 tbsp vegetable or groundnut oil	175 g/6 oz creamed coconut, chopped coarsely	400 g/14 oz canned straw mushrooms, drained
bunch of spring onions, chopped	2 tbsp red curry paste	350 g/12 oz large cooked peeled prawns
2 garlic cloves, chopped finely	450 ml/¾ pint fish stock	boiled jasmine rice, to serve
	2 tbsp fish sauce	
	2 tbsp Thai soy sauce	
	6 sprigs fresh Thai basil	

Heat the oil in a wok and stir-fry the spring onions and garlic for 2–3 minutes. Add the creamed coconut, red curry paste and stock and heat gently until the coconut has dissolved.

Stir in the fish sauce and soy sauce, then add the basil, mushrooms and prawns. Gradually bring to the boil and serve immediately with jasmine rice.

simple stir-fried scallops

SAUCE
2 tbsp lemon juice
2 tbsp soy sauce
1 tbsp honey
1 tbsp minced fresh root
  ginger
1 tbsp fish sauce,
  optional

1 clove garlic, peeled and
  flattened
STIR-FRY
450 g/1 lb scallops
2 tbsp sesame oil
1 tbsp chopped fresh
  coriander

1 tbsp chopped flat-leaf
  parsley
rice noodles, to serve

Combine the lemon juice, soy sauce, honey, ginger, fish sauce and garlic in a bowl and stir well to dissolve the honey. Add the scallops and toss to coat.

Heat a heavy frying pan or wok over the highest heat for 3 minutes. Add the oil and heat for 30 seconds.

Add the scallops with their sauce and the coriander and parsley to the pan. Stir constantly, cooking for about 3 minutes (less time if the scallops are smaller).

Serve immediately over rice noodles.

beef
& pork

Stir-frying beef and pork is one of the quickest ways of cooking these meats – and one of the tastiest and healthiest, too. If you favour Thai flavours, you can choose Thai Marinated Beef with Celery. If you prefer, you can choose Chinese dishes, such as Szechuan-style Pork & Pepper or Chinese-style Marinated Beef with Vegetables. But whatever your taste, there's something here for everyone.

EASY　　 SERVES 4　　 12 MINUTES +
30 MINUTES TO
MARINATE　　🕐 6 MINUTES

chinese-style marinated beef with vegetables

MARINADE
1 tbsp dry sherry
½ tbsp soy sauce
½ tbsp cornflour
½ tsp caster sugar
2 garlic cloves, chopped
   finely
1 tbsp sesame oil

STIR-FRY
500 g/1 lb 2 oz rump
   steak, cut into thin
   strips
3 tbsp sesame oil
½ tbsp soy sauce
½ tbsp cornflour
1 head of broccoli,
   cut into florets

2 carrots, cut into thin
   strips
125 g/4 oz mangetouts
125 ml/4 fl oz beef stock
250 g/9 oz baby spinach,
   shredded
cooked white rice or
   noodles, to serve

To make the marinade, mix the sherry, soy sauce, cornflour, sugar, garlic and sesame oil in a bowl. Add the beef to the mixture, cover with clingfilm and set aside to marinate for 30 minutes.

Heat 1 tablespoon of the sesame oil in a frying pan or wok. Stir-fry the beef without its marinade for 2 minutes until medium-rare. Discard the marinade. Remove the beef from the pan and set aside.

Combine the cornflour and soy sauce in a bowl and set aside. Pour the remaining 2 tablespoons of sesame oil into the pan, add the broccoli, carrots and mangetouts and stir-fry for 2 minutes.

Add the stock, cover the pan and steam for one minute. Stir in the spinach, beef and the cornflour mixture. Cook until the juices boil and thicken.

Serve over white rice or noodles.

VERY EASY   **SERVES 4**   **12 MINUTES +
1–2 HOURS TO
MARINATE**   **12 MINUTES**

pork with basil & lemon grass

MARINADE
1 stalk lemongrass, sliced
  finely
2 tbsp fish sauce,
  optional
4 tbsp fresh basil,
  shredded
juice of 1 lime

STIR-FRY
350 g/12 oz pork
  tenderloin, cubed
2 tbsp sesame oil
280 g/10 oz mushrooms,
  sliced thinly
1 courgette, sliced thinly
2 carrots, sliced thinly
115 g/4 oz canned
  bamboo shoots

115 g/4 oz canned water
  chestnuts, sliced thinly
1 garlic clove, crushed
125 ml/4 fl oz chicken
  stock
wedges of lime, to
  garnish
cooked basmati rice,
  to serve

Mix the lemon grass, fish sauce (if desired), basil and lime juice in a
bowl. Stir in the pork and toss well to coat. Cover with clingfilm and
refrigerate for 1–2 hours.

Heat 1 tablespoon of the oil in a frying pan or wok over a medium heat.
Add the meat and the marinade and stir-fry until the pork is browned.
Remove from the pan, set aside and keep warm.

Add the remaining 1 tablespoon of oil to the pan and heat. Add all the
vegetables and the garlic and stir-fry for about 3 minutes.

Return the pork to the pan and add the chicken stock. Cook for
5 minutes until the stock is reduced.

Transfer the stir-fry to warm serving dishes and garnish with wedges of
lime. Serve with the basmati rice.

VERY EASY   **SERVES 4**   **10 MINUTES +
1 HOUR TO
MARINATE**   🕐 **12 MINUTES**

hot & spicy beef with toasted pine nuts

MARINADE
2 tbsp soy sauce
1 tbsp cornflour
1 tbsp water
STIR-FRY
450 g/1 lb rump steak,
  cut into thin strips
55 g/2 oz pine nuts

1 lime, juiced
1 tbsp soy sauce
2 tbsp white wine vinegar
1 tsp cornflour
2 tbsp groundnut oil
3 tsp grated fresh root
  ginger
2 red, hot chillies,
  chopped finely

4 small baby leeks, halved
2 carrots, sliced thinly
100 g/3½ oz fine tip
  asparagus
3 shallots, sliced thinly
cooked noodles, to serve

To make the marinade, mix the soy sauce with the cornflour and water in a medium bowl. Add the beef and stir until the meat is well coated. Cover the bowl with clingfilm and chill in the refrigerator for 1 hour. Spread the pine nuts on a baking sheet and toast under a grill.

Mix the lime juice, the soy sauce, the vinegar, cornflour and 1 tablespoon of the groundnut oil in a small bowl and set aside. Heat the remaining groundnut oil in a large frying pan or wok. Stir-fry the ginger, chillies and leek for 2 minutes. Add the beef and the marinade and stir-fry for a further minute.

Stir in the carrots, asparagus and shallots and fry for 7 minutes or until the beef is cooked through. Add the lime mixture, reduce the heat and simmer until the liquid thickens. Remove from the heat, sprinkle with the pine nuts and serve.

VERY EASY   SERVES 4   10 MINUTES +
30 MINUTES TO
MARINATE   12 MINUTES

szechuan-style pork & pepper

MARINADE
1 tbsp soy sauce
pinch of chilli flakes
STIR-FRY
500 g/1 lb 2 oz pork
   tenderloin, cubed
2 tbsp cornflour

3 tbsp soy sauce
1 tbsp white wine vinegar
250 ml/9 fl oz water
2 tbsp groundnut oil
2 leeks, sliced thinly
1 red pepper, cut into
   thin strips

1 courgette, cut into thin
   strips
1 carrot, cut into thin
   strips
pinch of salt
cooked wild rice, to serve

To make the marinade, mix the soy sauce and chilli flakes in a bowl. Add the pork cubes and toss to coat. Cover with clingfilm and leave to stand for 30 minutes.

Combine the cornflour, soy sauce and white wine vinegar in a small bowl. Stir in the water gradually, then set aside.

Heat 1 tablespoon of the oil in a wok or frying pan. Add the pork and marinade mixture and stir-fry for 2–3 minutes. Remove the pork from the pan with a slotted spoon and set aside.

Heat the remaining oil in the pan, add the leeks and red pepper and stir-fry for 2 minutes. Then add the courgette, carrot and salt and stir-fry for 2 more minutes.

Stir in the pork and the cornflour mixture and bring to the boil, stirring constantly until the sauce thickens. Remove from the heat.

Serve immediately with cooked wild rice.

VERY EASY　 **SERVES 4**　◉ **10 MINUTES**　🕐 **10 MINUTES**

hot sesame beef

500 g/1 lb 2 oz beef
  fillet, cut into thin strips
1½ tbsp sesame seeds
125 ml/4 fl oz beef stock
2 tbsp soy sauce
2 tbsp grated fresh root
  ginger

2 garlic cloves, chopped
  finely
1 tsp cornflour
½ tsp chilli flakes
3 tbsp sesame oil
1 large head of broccoli,
  cut into florets

1 orange pepper, sliced
  thinly
1 red chilli, deseeded and
  sliced finely
1 tbsp chilli oil, to taste
1 tbsp chopped fresh
  coriander, to garnish
cooked wild rice, to serve

Mix the beef strips with 1 tablespoon of the sesame seeds in a small bowl. In a separate bowl, whisk together the beef stock, soy sauce, ginger, garlic, cornflour and chilli flakes.

Heat 1 tablespoon of the sesame oil in a large frying pan or wok. Stir-fry the beef strips for 2–3 minutes. Remove and set aside.

Discard any remaining oil in the pan, then wipe with kitchen paper to remove any stray sesame seeds. Heat the remaining oil, add the broccoli, orange pepper, chilli and chilli oil (if desired) and stir-fry for 2–3 minutes. Stir in the beef stock mixture, cover and simmer for 2 minutes.

Return the beef to the pan and simmer until the juices thicken, stirring occasionally. Cook for another 1–2 minutes.

Sprinkle with the remaining sesame seeds. Serve over cooked wild rice and garnish with fresh coriander.

quick pork & pasta stir-fry

1 tbsp groundnut oil
½ tsp chilli powder, or to
  taste
2 garlic cloves, crushed
½ red cabbage, shredded

8 small baby leeks, halved
1 orange pepper, sliced
  thinly
1 carrot, sliced thinly
1 courgette, sliced thinly

350 g/12 oz pork
  tenderloin, cubed
cooked fettucine or
  vermicelli, to serve

Heat the oil in a large frying pan or wok over a medium heat and add
the chilli powder, garlic and red cabbage. Stir-fry for 2–3 minutes.

Stir in the rest of the vegetables and cook for a further 2 minutes. Add
the meat, increase the heat and stir-fry for about 5 minutes, or until the
pork is well cooked and the dish is piping hot.

Serve immediately over fettucine or vermicelli.

ginger beef with yellow peppers

MARINADE
2 tbsp soy sauce
2 tsp groundnut oil
1½ tsp caster sugar
1 tsp cornflour

STIR-FRY
500 g/1 lb 2 oz beef
  fillet, cut into
  2.5 cm/1 inch cubes
2 tsp groundnut oil
2 garlic cloves, crushed
2 tbsp grated fresh root
  ginger

pinch of chilli flakes
2 yellow peppers, sliced
  thinly
125 g/4½ oz baby corn
175 g/6 oz mangetouts
hot noodles drizzled with
  sesame oil, to serve

To make the marinade, mix the soy sauce, groundnut oil, sugar and cornflour in a bowl. Stir in the beef cubes, then cover with clingfilm and set aside to marinate for 30 minutes.

Heat the groundnut oil in a frying pan or wok over a medium heat. Add the garlic, ginger and chilli flakes and cook for 30 seconds. Stir in the yellow peppers and baby corn, and stir-fry for 2 minutes. Add the mangetouts and cook for another minute.

Remove the vegetables from the pan. Put the beef cubes and marinade into the pan and stir-fry for 3–4 minutes or until cooked to taste. Return the vegetables to the pan, mix well and cook until all the ingredients are heated through.

Remove from the heat and serve over noodles.

 EXTREMELY EASY  SERVES 4   10 MINUTES +
1 HOUR TO
MARINATE   6 MINUTES

thai marinated beef with celery

MARINADE
1 tsp salt
2 tbsp fish sauce
STIR-FRY
500 g/1 lb 2 oz beef
   fillet, cut into thin strips

3 celery stalks, cut into
   2.5 cm/1 inch batons
1 red pepper, cut into
   thin strips
1 red chilli, seeds
   removed, sliced finely

250 ml/9 fl oz vegetable
   oil
extra fish sauce, to serve
lime quarters, to garnish

To make the marinade, mix the salt and fish sauce in a large bowl.
Add the beef and toss to coat. Cover with clingfilm and put in the
refrigerator for 1 hour to marinate.

Heat the oil in the pan and deep-fry the beef over a medium heat for
2–3 minutes until crispy. Remove the pan from the heat and, using a
slotted spoon, lift out the meat and drain it on kitchen paper. Discard
all but 2 tablespoons of the oil.

Heat the remaining oil in the pan and stir-fry the celery, red pepper and
chilli for 1 minute. Add the beef and cook until hot.

Serve with extra fish sauce and garnish with lime.

sweet & sour pork

150 ml/5 fl oz vegetable oil, for deep-frying
225 g/8 oz pork fillet, cut into 1-cm/½-inch cubes
1 onion, sliced
1 green pepper, seeded and sliced
225 g/8 oz pineapple pieces
1 small carrot, cut into thin strips

25 g/1 oz canned bamboo shoots, drained, rinsed and halved
rice or noodles, to serve

BATTER
125 g/4½ oz plain flour
1 tbsp cornflour
1½ tsp baking powder
1 tbsp vegetable oil

SAUCE
125 g/4½ oz light brown sugar
2 tbsp cornflour
125 ml/4 fl oz white wine vinegar
2 garlic cloves, crushed
4 tbsp tomato purée
6 tbsp pineapple juice

To make the batter, sift the plain flour into a mixing bowl, together with the cornflour and baking powder. Add the vegetable oil and stir in enough water to make a thick, smooth batter (about 175 ml/6 fl oz).

Pour the vegetable oil into a preheated wok and heat until almost smoking.

Dip the cubes of pork into the batter, and cook in the hot oil, in batches, until the pork is cooked through. Remove the pork from the wok with a slotted spoon and drain on kitchen paper. Set aside and keep warm until required.

Drain all but 1 tablespoon of oil from the wok and return it to the heat. Add the onion, pepper, pineapple pieces, carrot and bamboo shoots and stir-fry for 1–2 minutes. Remove from the wok with a slotted spoon and set aside.

Mix all of the sauce ingredients together and pour into the wok. Bring to the boil, stirring until thickened and clear. Cook for 1 minute, then return the pork and vegetables to the wok. Cook for a further 1–2 minutes, then transfer to a serving plate and serve with rice or noodles.

vegetable
dishes

Vegetables retain their crunchy freshness when they are stir-fried, and their natural healthy taste can be quickly enhanced with delicious simple and exotic sauces. From Oyster Mushrooms & Vegetables with Peanut Chilli Sauce and Spicy Indian Vegetarian Stir-fry through to Stir-fried Japanese Noodles, there is a great selection of main and side dishes here to tantalise all taste buds.

stir-fried japanese noodles

225 g/8 oz Japanese egg
  noodles
2 tbsp sunflower oil
1 red onion, sliced
1 garlic clove, crushed

500 g/1 lb 2 oz mixed
  mushrooms, such as
  shiitake, oyster and
  brown cap
350 g/12 oz pak choi

2 tbsp sweet sherry
6 tbsp soy sauce
4 spring onions, sliced
1 tbsp sesame seeds,
  toasted

Place the noodles in a large bowl, pour over enough boiling water to
cover and leave to soak for 10 minutes. Heat the oil in a large,
preheated wok.

Add the red onion and garlic to the wok and stir-fry for 2–3 minutes,
or until softened. Add the mushrooms to the wok and stir-fry for
5 minutes, or until softened. Drain the noodles and add to the wok.

Add the pak choi, sweet sherry and soy sauce to the wok and toss
to mix well. Stir-fry for 2–3 minutes, or until the liquid is just bubbling.
Transfer the noodle mixture to warmed serving bowls, sprinkle with
sliced spring onions and toasted sesame seeds and serve immediately.

VERY EASY   **SERVES 4**   ⬛ **10 MINUTES**   🕐 **15 MINUTES**

spicy indian vegetarian stir-fry

3 tbsp vegetable oil
½ tsp turmeric
225 g/8 oz potatoes,
   cut into 1 cm/½ inch
   cubes
3 shallots, chopped finely
1 bay leaf
½ tsp ground cumin

1 tsp finely grated fresh
   root ginger
¼ tsp chilli powder
4 tomatoes, chopped
   roughly
300 g/10½ oz spinach
   (de-stalked), chopped
   roughly

125 g/4½ oz fresh or
   frozen peas
1 tbsp lemon juice
salt and pepper
cooked basmati rice,
   to serve

In a large frying pan or wok, heat 2 tablespoons of the oil and add the turmeric and a pinch of salt. Carefully add the potatoes, stirring continuously to coat in the turmeric. Stir-fry for 5 minutes, remove from the pan and set aside.

Heat the remaining tablespoon of oil and stir-fry the shallots for 1–2 minutes. Mix in the bay leaf, cumin, ginger and chilli powder, then add the tomatoes and stir-fry for two minutes.

Add the spinach, mixing well to combine all the flavours. Cover and simmer for 2–3 minutes. Return the potatoes to the pan and add the peas and lemon juice. Cook for 5 minutes or until the potatoes are tender.

Remove the pan from the heat, discard the bay leaf and season with salt and pepper. Serve with cooked basmati rice.

classic stir-fried vegetables

3 tbsp sesame oil
8 spring onions, chopped finely
1 garlic clove, crushed
1 tbsp grated fresh root ginger
1 head of broccoli, cut into florets

1 orange or yellow pepper, chopped roughly
125 g/4½ oz red cabbage, shredded
125 g/4½ oz baby sweetcorn
175 g/6 oz portobello or large cup mushrooms, sliced thinly

200 g/7 oz fresh beansprouts
250 g/9 oz canned water chestnuts, drained
4 tsp soy sauce
cooked wild rice, to serve

Heat 2 tablespoons of the oil in a large frying pan or wok over a high heat. Stir-fry six of the spring onions, with the garlic and ginger for 30 seconds.

Add the broccoli, pepper and red cabbage and stir-fry for 1–2 minutes. Mix in the baby sweetcorn and mushrooms and stir-fry for a further 1–2 minutes.

Finally, add the beansprouts and water chestnuts and cook for another 2 minutes. Pour in the soy sauce to taste and stir well.

Transfer to warm dishes and serve immediately over cooked wild rice, and garnish with remaining spring onions.

julienne vegetable salad

4 tbsp vegetable or
  groundnut oil
225 g/8 oz tofu with
  herbs, cubed
1 red onion, sliced
4 spring onions, cut into
  5-cm/2-inch lengths
1 garlic clove, chopped
2 carrots, cut into
  matchsticks

115 g/4 oz fine French
  beans, trimmed
1 yellow pepper, deseeded
  and cut into strips
115 g/4 oz broccoli, cut
  into florets
1 large courgette, cut
  into matchsticks
50 g/2 oz beansprouts

2 tbsp red curry paste
4 tbsp Thai soy sauce
1 tbsp rice wine vinegar
1 tsp palm sugar or soft,
  light brown sugar
few Thai basil leaves
350 g/12 oz rice
  vermicelli noodles

Heat the oil in a wok or large frying pan and fry the tofu cubes for
3–4 minutes, until browned on all sides. Lift out of the oil and drain on
kitchen paper.

Add the onions, garlic and carrots to the hot oil and fry for 1–2 minutes
before adding the rest of the vegetables, except for the beansprouts.
Stir-fry for 2–3 minutes. Add the beansprouts, then stir in the curry
paste, soy, vinegar, sugar and basil leaves. Cook for 30 seconds.

Soak the noodles in boiling water or stock for 2–3 minutes (check the
packet instructions) or until tender and drain well.

Pile the vegetables on to the noodles, and serve topped with the tofu
cubes. Garnish with extra basil if liked.

VERY EASY   **SERVES 4**   **10 MINUTES +
20 MINUTES TO
MARINATE**   ◷ **10 MINUTES**

spicy tofu

MARINADE
75 ml/2½ fl oz vegetable
  stock
2 tsp cornflour
2 tbsp soy sauce
1 tbsp caster sugar
pinch of chilli flakes

STIR-FRY
250 g/9 oz firm tofu,
  rinsed and drained
  thoroughly and cut into
  1 cm/½ inch cubes
4 tbsp groundnut oil
1 tbsp grated fresh root
  ginger
3 garlic cloves, crushed

4 spring onions, sliced
  thinly
1 head of broccoli, cut
  into florets
1 carrot, cut into batons
1 yellow pepper, sliced
  thinly
250 g/9 oz shiitake
  mushrooms, sliced thinly
steamed rice, to serve

Blend the vegetable stock, cornflour, soy sauce, sugar and chilli flakes
together in a large bowl. Add the tofu and toss well to cover in the
marinade. Set aside to marinate for 20 minutes.

In a large frying pan or wok, heat 2 tablespoons of the groundnut oil
and stir-fry the tofu with its marinade until brown and crispy. Remove
from the pan and set aside.

Heat the remaining 2 tablespoons of groundnut oil in the pan and
stir-fry the ginger, garlic and spring onions for 30 seconds. Add the
broccoli, carrot, yellow pepper and mushrooms to the pan and cook for
5–6 minutes. Return the tofu to the pan and stir-fry to reheat. Serve
immediately over steamed rice.

VERY EASY   **SERVES 4**   🥄 **10 MINUTES**   🕐 **6 MINUTES**

oyster mushrooms & vegetables with peanut chilli sauce

1 tbsp sesame oil	450 g/1 lb oyster	wedges of lime, to garnish
4 spring onions, sliced	mushrooms, sliced thinly	cooked rice or noodles,
finely	2 tbsp coarse peanut	to serve
1 carrot, cut into batons	butter	
1 courgette, cut into	1 tsp chilli powder,	
batons	or to taste	
½ head of broccoli,	3 tbsp water	
cut into florets		

Heat the oil in a frying pan or wok until almost smoking. Stir-fry the spring onions for 1 minute. Add the carrot and courgette and stir-fry for another minute. Then add the broccoli and cook for one more minute.

Stir in the mushrooms and cook until they are soft and at least half the liquid they produce has evaporated. Add the peanut butter and stir well. Season with the chilli powder to taste. Finally, add the water and cook for a further minute.

Garnish with wedges of lime and serve with rice or noodles.

stir-fried broccoli

2 tbsp vegetable oil
2 medium heads of
   broccoli, cut into florets
2 tbsp soy sauce

1 tsp cornflour
1 tbsp caster sugar
1 tsp grated fresh root
   ginger

1 garlic clove, crushed
pinch of hot chilli flakes
1 tsp toasted sesame
   seeds, to garnish

In a large frying pan or wok, heat the oil until almost smoking. Stir-fry the broccoli for 4–5 minutes.

In a small bowl, combine the soy sauce, cornflour, sugar, ginger, garlic and hot chilli flakes. Add the mixture to the broccoli. Cook over a gentle heat, stirring constantly, for 2–3 minutes until the sauce thickens slightly.

Transfer to a serving dish, garnish with the sesame seeds and serve immediately.

index